When you need more advice

It does happen that even with the help of your pre-law advisor, law school counselor and your parents that you just are lost. That's OK. If you are uncertain about what you are doing or why you are doing it, or if you simply want more help in any way, visit https://linktr.ee/legallearningcenter

This link will take you to all the ways The Legal Learning Center, Inc. can help you with your legal journey. From social media connecting, to free handouts to The Legal Learning Podcast and The Pre-Law Survival Guide - all focused on helping prospective law students save time, money and stress on their legal journey.

Best wishes on YOUR legal journey!

It's important
to stay motivated!

Add your favorite inspiring and motivating quotes

Skill + habit = Success" - Mike Kim - LSAT Trainer

"Always bear in mind that your own resolution to succeed is more important than any one thing".
- Abraham Lincoln

If you are considering applying to law school, then this is the journal for you. This journal will guide you through the application process. It will prompt you with deadlines and checklists to ensure you have remembered all that you should, have submitted all that you should and have considered all that you should. However, no list is exhaustive so there is plenty of room for personalization as well. If at all possible, give yourself a year to begin planning your application process.

My name is

_____

And this is my
Pre-Law Journal

I plan to start law school in

_____

My ***dream*** school is

_____

ISBN: 979-8-9853837-1-3

Rough Timeline

September - November (1 year before apps open):

- ☐ Speak to law/grad advisor at your school
- ☐ Attend law fairs, network, conduct informational interviews
- ☐ Compile list of desired schools, programs and stats
- ☐ Develop relationships with 2-3 professors that you'll feel comfortable asking for letters of recommendation

December - March:

- ☐ Visit www.LSAC.org
- ☐ Sign up for Credential Assembly Services (CAS)
- ☐ Sign up for Candidate Referral Service (CRS)
- ☐ Take a diagnostic test (free on Khan Academy)
- ☐ Take note of fee waiver or accommodation rules and deadlines
- ☐ Keep track of LSAT registration deadlines on LSAC website
- ☐ Devise a study plan (self-study, tutor or course)

Rough Timeline

March - July:

☐ Take the LSAT (decide if you need to take it again)

☐ Purchase CAS

August - November:

☐ Upload all necessary documents to LSAC

☐ Submit applications

Documents that need to be in LSAC

- [ ] LSAT scores(s)
  (automatically uploaded 4 weeks post test)

- [ ] Undergrad transcripts
  (ALL institutions)

- [ ] Letters of recommendation
  (Send request directly to 2-3 people through LSAC)

- [ ] Applications

Documents to be uploaded to school specific apps

☐ Resume (different than professional resume)

☐ Personal Statement (Check the prompt for EACH school)

☐ Diversity Statement (If applicable. Check the prompt at EACH school.)

☐ Any other school specific essays.

☐ Addendum

LSAT Plan

---◆●◆---

I intend to study for the LSAT with _____.

The cost will be _____.

Study start date _____.

Number of hours per week _____.

LSAT test date _____.

Test registration date _____.

The cost is _____.

Request test accommodations by _____.

Test location is _____.

I will receive my results by _____.

Notes:

LSAT Strategy

How many times you can or should take the LSAT can vary from year to year, so make sure you have researched the most current recommendations approximately one year before you plan to take the LSAT. This will give you enough time to take a course and re-take the exam if you decide that is in your best interest.

For general LSAT info visit:
www.lsac.org/lsat/taking-lsat

My favorite LSAT podcasts:
LSAT Unplugged + Law School Admission Test

LSAT Score Analysis

You took the LSAT, now what? First, congrats! But keep in mind there may be times where you will want to cancel or re-take the exam. If re-taking the exam is a possibility for you based on your timeline and the LSAT rules at the time you are applying, here's a few ways to evaluate whether you should re-take the exam.

How far into the application process are you, do you really think you can change your score, do you have a plan to improve your score, how did you feel as you took the test, did the score accurately reflect your abilities?

You should only cancel a score if you pretty much know something went very wrong (you were sick, left early) or if the LSAT decides to return to the system in which your scores are averaged which would mean you really only want your best score on record.

Transcripts

Be sure you obtain transcripts for every college you have attended. Don't forget about that summer school class you took a few years ago, the study abroad program you did or any other units you have from other places. Every unit counts!

I attended _____ schools since high school. Those schools are:

1.
2.
3.
4.

I have obtained transcripts from:

1.
2.
3.
4.

Personal Statement

This can take months to perfect. Start early!

If you are a junior, start as soon as your junior year ends and the LSAT is over (although if you have time, it can't hurt to start sooner).

Possible topics:

1.

2.

3.

4.

5.

6.

Diversity Statement

---◆•◆---

This can take months to perfect as well, so again, start early!

Diverse can mean many things so this should always be a consideration. Possible things that make you diverse: culture, socio-economics, race, gender, special needs. Check the school requirements. Some schools have strict guidelines.

Possible topics:

1.

2.

3.

4.

5.

6.

Essay Links

Personal Statement
https://bit.ly/3GobS84

https://bit.ly/3HXce5U

Diversity Statement
https://bit.ly/31UOLTC

https://bit.ly/3K8U5Uv

https://bit.ly/3zTFFmL

Addendum
https://bit.ly/3nky8IB

Letters of Recommendation

Building connections with professors and other potential recommenders is important, but maintaining the connection is essential. Consider sending a "thank you" to a professor shortly after a course is completed to stand out in their memory. This is especially important if there will be a gap between taking that class and applying for law school.

Keep in mind that sometimes it can take months to receive a letter of recommendation. People are busy and forget. You may have follow up or even ask someone else instead.

To allow the recommender plenty of time to write the letter and allow you time to find a back-up person, if necessary, you should ask for letters of recommendation at least three months in advance of submitting applications to law school.

If you are applying to law school early fall, and you are requesting letters from professors you know in the spring, ask those professors in the spring. Don't wait until summer when you might lose that connection. Ideally you will have 1-2 of your recommenders be professors.

Individual I will ask for a LOR:

_____

Date I will ask for LOR _____
Date of follow up: _____
Date obtained: _____

Individual I will ask for a LOR:

_____

Date I will ask for LOR _____
Date of follow up: _____
Date obtained: _____

Individual I will ask for a LOR:

_____

Date I will ask for LOR _____
Date of follow up: _____
Date obtained: _____

Individual I will ask for a LOR:

_____

Date I will ask for LOR _____
Date of follow up: _____
Date obtained: _____

Resume

Most colleges offer free assistance with resume writing. Ask your pre-law advisor where to go if you are uncertain. However, if you are not currently in college or unable to go to a workshop, the internet is full of examples. Keep in mind that there are a few key differences between a regular resume and one for law school applications.

For a few samples visit:

https://bit.ly/3K86tnZ

Applications

Many schools do not have firm due dates for their applications, or have due dates that are far past when you should apply. For most schools, fall is the time to apply, even if due dates are in spring. If you apply later in the cycle, your chance to get into a school or receive a good money offer may be diminished. Always check out the applications as soon as possible. Some schools ask "extra" questions in their applications that may take you extra time to complete. You don't want this to delay your submission so take a look at all applications before you are ready to apply so you know what to expect.

Application Submissions

School: _____
Application fee: _____
Application due date: _____
Date I will submit my application: _____
Response: _____

School: _____
Application fee: _____
Application due date: _____
Date I will submit my application: _____
Response: _____

School: _____
Application fee: _____
Application due date: _____
Date I will submit my application: _____
Response: _____

School: _____
Application fee: _____
Application due date: _____
Date I will submit my application: _____
Response: _____

Application Submissions

School: _____

Application fee: _____

Application due date: _____

Date I will submit my application: _____

Response: _____

School: _____

Application fee: _____

Application due date: _____

Date I will submit my application: _____

Response: _____

School: _____

Application fee: _____

Application due date: _____

Date I will submit my application: _____

Response: _____

School: _____

Application fee: _____

Application due date: _____

Date I will submit my application: _____

Response: _____

Application Submissions

School: _____

Application fee: _____

Application due date: _____

Date I will submit my application: _____

Response: _____

School: _____

Application fee: _____

Application due date: _____

Date I will submit my application: _____

Response: _____

School: _____

Application fee: _____

Application due date: _____

Date I will submit my application: _____

Response: _____

School: _____

Application fee: _____

Application due date: _____

Date I will submit my application: _____

Response: _____

Essays

———————◆●◄———————

School: _____

- ☐ Personal Statement
- ☐ Diversity Statement
- ☐ Extra Essay
- ☐ Addendum

School: _____

- ☐ Personal Statement
- ☐ Diversity Statement
- ☐ Extra Essay
- ☐ Addendum

School: _____

- ☐ Personal Statement
- ☐ Diversity Statement
- ☐ Extra Essay
- ☐ Addendum

Essays

———————◆●◆———————

School: _____

- [ ] Personal Statement
- [ ] Diversity Statement
- [ ] Extra Essay
- [ ] Addendum

School: _____

- [ ] Personal Statement
- [ ] Diversity Statement
- [ ] Extra Essay
- [ ] Addendum

School: _____

- [ ] Personal Statement
- [ ] Diversity Statement
- [ ] Extra Essay
- [ ] Addendum

Essays

———————◄●►———————

School: _____

- ☐ Personal Statement
- ☐ Diversity Statement
- ☐ Extra Essay
- ☐ Addendum

School: _____

- ☐ Personal Statement
- ☐ Diversity Statement
- ☐ Extra Essay
- ☐ Addendum

School: _____

- ☐ Personal Statement
- ☐ Diversity Statement
- ☐ Extra Essay
- ☐ Addendum

Essays

School: _____

- ☐ Personal Statement
- ☐ Diversity Statement
- ☐ Extra Essay
- ☐ Addendum

School: _____

- ☐ Personal Statement
- ☐ Diversity Statement
- ☐ Extra Essay
- ☐ Addendum

School: _____

- ☐ Personal Statement
- ☐ Diversity Statement
- ☐ Extra Essay
- ☐ Addendum

Notes on
Financial Aid Options
and Money Considerations

Notes on Financial Aid Options and Money Considerations

Notes on Financial Aid Options and Money Considerations

Questions for my pre-law advisor

Questions for my
pre-law advisor

Questions for my
pre-law advisor

Ranking Law Schools

Rank the law schools to which you are applying, using the following pages, in order of preference prior to receipt of acceptance/denial letters. This helps to avoid accepting a school simply because they have accepted you. If a school accepts you and they are at the bottom of your list, seeing them listed at the bottom will prompt you to confirm whether you really want to go. Law school is expensive; go on YOUR terms, not necessarily theirs.

1.
2.
3.
4.
5.
6.
7.
8.
9.
10.
11.
12.

Law School Application Checklist

Use the following chart to help compare the schools you are considering. You don't have to rank your choices exactly, but it's a good idea to compare them and place a relative value on each school. Feel free to add additional sections. Additional sections should be anything that may influence your decision. With this chart, more than one school may share a ranking or grade; that's OK.

You will need to create a scoring system that works for you. You can award each column an A through F, like grades, or a score which can be 1 through 3 or 1 through 10, or any other creation that works for you. Whatever makes sense so you can see how you really feel about a school, when it's all added up.

Comparison Chart

For a larger chart visit you can edit:
https://bit.ly/3ucSCHu

School							
Tuition							
Location							
Money Offer							
Travel home							
Daily travel							
Programs							
Cost of living							
Score							

Special Factors to Consider for Each School

Is there something special that doesn't technically factor into your calculations? Something you just want to note on the side? Perhaps the fact that it's a really pretty campus? Maybe that's not worth listing in your comparison chart and giving a technical value, but it's something you want to list so that when you make your final comparison, you don't forget it. List it here.

Special Factors to Consider

Choosing a School

I have been accepted to _____

Their tuition is _____

Cost of living there is _____
(housing, transportation, etc)

Other costs of going there may include _____

_____

(ex: flying home)

I have been accepted to _____

Their tuition is _____

Cost of living there is _____
(housing, transportation, etc)

Other costs of going there may include _____

_____

(ex: flying home)

Choosing a School

I have been accepted to _____

Their tuition is _____

Cost of living there is _____
(housing, transportation, etc)

Other costs of going there may include _____

_____

(ex: flying home)

I have been accepted to _____

Their tuition is _____

Cost of living there is _____
(housing, transportation, etc)

Other costs of going there may include _____

_____

(ex: flying home)

Choosing a School

———————◆•◆———————

I have been accepted to _____

Their tuition is _____

Cost of living there is _____
(housing, transportation, etc)

Other costs of going there may include _____

_____

(ex: flying home)

I have been accepted to _____

Their tuition is _____

Cost of living there is _____
(housing, transportation, etc)

Other costs of going there may include _____

_____

(ex: flying home)

Law School Counselors

I recommend you find the name and contact information for a law school counselor at each school to which you are applying so you can readily ask questions as they arise. You should contact a law school counselor at each school to which you have been accepted, if you have not already contacted them during the application process. A few questions you may want to ask include: How active is the student body in clubs and organizations? Which legal fraternities are active on that campus and how active are they? What are their recommendations for success at that school?

School   Name   Contact info

_____

_____

_____

_____

Law School Counselors

School	Name	Contact info

Notes

Notes

Notes

Notes

Notes

Notes

Notes

Notes

Notes

Notes

Notes

www.ingramcontent.com/pod-product-compliance
Lightning Source LLC
Chambersburg PA
CBHW070452130626
46553CB00006B/2368